Seeds on my Chin

and Selected Poems

Rudy Martinez Jr.

The Art of Labor PLLC

Seeds on my Chin

CONTENTS

Part I – Watercolors

Seeds on My Chin 2

Tag 3

October Breeze 4

Tortilla Therapy 5

Scars 7

Lunch Special #7 8

Sediment 9

Desert Ravine 11

Country Cottage Window 13

Learning for the Licensed 14

CONTENTS

Hill Country Landscapes 16

My First Beer in High School Goes Bad 18

Part II - The Pause Chronicles

Tending My Garden 22

Tortilla Shrine of Our Lady of Los Apaches Café 23

Pain Demands We Laugh 25

Dead Grackle Directions 27

Walk Away 28

Bedtime Story 30

Pointing Chins 32

Incoherent Dreams 34

Laundry Day 36

Concert for Kites 37

St. Paddy's Day 38

CONTENTS

Sauntering on Smith St.   39

Three Lines   41

Lawns, Dogs and Refried Beans   42

Part III - The Grace Escape

The Flavor of Gin   46

Color of Memory   47

No One to Blame   49

Depression for Dessert   51

Closet Space   53

Empty Kiss   54

Disposable Love Song   55

Ambition   56

migraine shuffle   58

While I Wait   60

Wet Sand Fingerprints   61

CONTENTS

Bandages   63

Part IV - Faith is a Verb

The Resolute Dawn   66

Patron Saint of Broken Vows   67

Day of the Dead Moon   69

House of Prayer   71

Seed of Praise   72

Picnic Bench Constellation   74

Under Tall Trees   76

Kristin   78

See, Hear and Feel   80

Labor and Prayer   82

ACKNOWLEDGEMENTS   85
ABOUT THE AUTHOR   87
NOTES   89

Front and back cover design by Rudy Martinez Jr.

The Art of Labor
Spring, Texas 77386

Art of Labor logo
Apple Specialty
Advertising

First Printing, 2021

for Kristin

Part I – Watercolors

Seeds on My Chin

Clouds soak up the sunset above a pecan tree canopy,
people scattered in the back yard in pockets of shade,
beads of sweat on brow and amber tumblers of lemonade.

Uncle Lalo rolls the metal Coca Cola cooler
to the thickest collection of emerald green grass,
watermelons bobbing in a pool of water and ice.

Mom pulls the first victim from the tub,
Dad approaches the picnic table, machete in hand.
Laughter and wet sugar oscillate like a chorus

from the back porch to the swings by the garage.
Cousins spit seeds at the neighbor's dog.
Stop that, the adults shout, annoyed by his bark,

chins lacquered with melon seed. The sun
slides to a different aspect, leaves us sticky
in shadows, gnarled rinds and mosquito bites.

Funny words, silly pictures.
sloppy floppy folly.
Kiss me. Kick me. Help me stand up.

Hands clench grass-green scented air.
Eyes mold red clay castles.
Shoulders wear cotton candy feathers.

Muscles quiver on the tenth episode
of ring-around-a-rosy.
Everyone falls down.

Young-lings giggle bubbles,
Undetected, like Mojave Desert showers.
like a fallen hackberry tree
in the Smoky Mountains.

October Breeze

Changing air arrives from next season's smile;
it lilts and teases, suggests the road north
not south, play games, fight in the grass,
pull twigs from dead branches, click-clack on iron rails.
Heat tries to squelch the impulse.

Games the elixir of daydream desires.
To play tag, circle the playground,
to tickle, be tickled, laugh until red in the face,
goose bumps up and down each arm,
exhausted from the in and out gasps
required to stay in the game.

The plague of duty requires resolve
as leaves tumble across the parking lot,
an October breeze invitation.

Tortilla Therapy

Blue flames tickle the kettle-black comal.
A pale-yellow Tupperware™ bowl
pulled from the refrigerator, dollops of dough
pinched from a pasty colored mound.
My grandmother squeezes smooth balls,
centers them on a wax-paper sheet.
Her rolling pin christens ball after ball

in Crisco and flour dust, each perfect
circle stacked beside blue-fingered flames.
The running faucet wets her fingers;
drops sprinkled like holy water
on the hot comal turn to beads, cumbia
three or four steps, hiss and evaporate.

Carne guisada filled for breakfast,
they revive sleepy steps, erase
the blues from summer-time chores.
A mid-morning snack, butter pools in dips
and cracks; she gives me two when I say
please. Bean and cheese stuffed for dinner,
peanut butter covered for dessert.

My tortillas, stuffed with sausage and eggs,
are store bought, heated on a Teflon™ pan.
My grandmother winces from the pedestal
of her last tortilla. They are not the version
she concocted before I was born. Substitutes
though, empower a delicate memory mist.
Salient, fragrant, sublime.

Scars

Glass door checkerboard explodes,
tendons and tissue tear, base of palm
to forearm. Blood gushes
through a clenched fist tourniquet.

Wound incubates in a cocoon bandage
for months. Must be explained
to sixth-grade teachers, uncles and aunts.

It was a fight, he says.
My brother slammed the door in my face.
Shame on you demon child.

Yes, I am hides behind
careful or I'll do it again.
His scars reach in a handshake,
fissures on his arm sternly warn;
remember - anger is quick,
forgiveness
exceedingly
slow.

Deep fried corn shells glisten like sand
on an Acapulco beach,
tender morsels of pork
seasoned by a mother's love,
artfully tucked between layers of crunch.

Chopped tomatoes and lettuce
spill into shredded cheese and melts
into neighboring rice and beans.
The lunch plate special in a state of grace.

Salsa, the hot variety, floods sinuses,
tears flow from pain, pleasure,
the sting of a pierced jalapeño seed.

Oh such delight,
three brother tacos
excite the palate
from first to final bite.

Sediment

Tim drives past rickety gates,
truck choked with gypsum board
and warped planks.
Diesel fumes, smoldering ash,
a dump's ghostly demeanor
the moment light breaches
the highest peak beyond the pit.

A carpenter, my grandfather
practiced his craft in homes
that brag of stained glass.

He enchants with stories,
lays ceramic tiles,
installs kitchen sink frames,
drills brass fitted cabinets.
Never forgets to say;
yes sir, thank you ma'am.

He shared his most sage advice
when we were alone in his truck;
When I was fifteen I used steamy hot water
and Ivory soap to wipe pimples from my face.

Use the bar I have in the garage,
I rub it on cabinet drawers
to make them slide instead of stick.

Other stories drip into consciousness
as I sit in the barrel where forgotten moment's pool,
retrieve wisdom like an extra cup of coffee
from an old pot's sediment.

Desert Ravine

In need of room under foot,
an expectant mother drives three sons
to the swimming pool down the street.
Impervious to danger, they wander,
dive headfirst, imitate dolphins at sea.

Sky changes hue between underwater dives,
blue haze to washed-out copper.
Kettledrum thunder signals lesson's end.
Lifeguards attempt to corral reluctant kids
below a shelter of charcoal canvas
stretched over widely spaced pine planks.

Saguaro cacti on either side of road
hold arms to sky,
unable to slow torrential sheets.
Ravine rushes with runoff,
voices on either side of gully shout.

A goat swaddled in prickly pear paddles
rides the surge of debris, sand and rain.
The oldest begins his leap of faith.
Uncoils his sapling muscle,

dives headfirst, falls on all fours
amidst a crowd of anonymous feet.

In the car, water puddles on vinyl seats.
Warm arms and thirsty towels revive cold skin.
The sun drags dark clouds beyond the horizon
as toads begin their nighttime song.

Country Cottage Window

A window opens
to crack the shell of day.
Fog rivers flood the pasture
in gray light, damp yawns.

Strong coffee and biscuits.
bottle of honey in the pantry,
a tin of raspberry tea.

Giant oaks huddle a country cottage.
Mossy cobblestone trail
welcomes neighbors, strangers,
a dog named Beau.

A bumble bee floats in and out,
buzzes my ear, aligns my sight.
The kitchen window reveals
blessings from the last ray of sun.
Now it's time for raspberry tea,
a dribble of honey just before I sleep.

Learning for the Licensed

Eight hundred accountants in tourist attire,
a lake of tables and chairs,
early session riddled by incidental acts,

A cricket sings on a stage of cold cement.
Woman in my line of sight, hacking cough,
spits every ten minutes into a paper cup.
Elderly man converses with young woman.
She, extremely tolerant or insincerely polite.

Recurring trumpet sneeze on my left
signals the season for allergic fits.
Some cross legs under tables, feet rock
cabaret style. Walls are flat maroon,
the only artwork the white on red exit signs.

Lectern lamp a beacon, ceiling lights dimmed.
Ambivalent audience ignores the lecture-hiss
heard from ceiling loudspeakers
a few decibels above the cricket's song.

Slides shuffle across a screen just before lunch;
the speaker pulls women's shoes from a box,

the props enthuse a few in the first three rows.
In row thirty-six, I close my binder,
join back of class group
in adjacent hall serving line.

Hill Country Landscapes

Wildflowers and screen doors decorate
the slope aimed at the hidden stream.
Brown sleeps under the sage bush,
no complaints, without shame,
another day convincing lavender
her blossoms speak to him by name.

An outdoor grill ribbons smoke
through tall trees, brisket grieves
for hot coals like a ghost
trapped by a daughter's laugh.

Envious shade conceals primal hues
with a somber-tipped brush. Red apples
lounge in a bowl while blue and yellow
use butterfly wings to paint the slope green.

A mockingbird perched on a high branch
shifts its pointed song from clouds
resembling Barcelona bulls
to neighbors poised
beyond the picket fence.

Blue and yellow avoid brown
crouched in the circle
shade rendered sacred.
Songbirds compose lullabies
in the high branches. The music
ribbons through sunflower fields,
along banks of the hidden stream.

My First Beer in High School Goes Bad

The popular mingle in the first act
as other performers gather on the porch,
curious, afraid, ready to ride
the summer night without a guide.

Music paves a way through front door.
Incense mingles with cigarette smoke,
black lights set posters and t-shirts aglow.

The story of lazy-eye Mike
and the head football coach;
funny, cruel, over done.

I skirt the fringe, bury a cringe
after the last sip of my first beer,
rise to hunt down something to eat.

The floor evaporates under me,
a circus high wire takes its place.
My steps miss their mark.
First comes the sofa then bounce
goes my head into a herd of feet.

Back from my audience with the pope,
the floor remarks –
Your performance was well played.
Rest a while,
they may need you for the closing act.

Part II - The Pause Chronicles

Tending My Garden

Hummingbirds avoid
my garden. They do not trust
the pigweed stink among
the skeletons of scarlet sage.

An herbal iced tea,
too pale to be taken seriously
as green, cools my urge
to pull weeds.

Pigeons dunk bird seed
in the pool of the bottle's dew,
fly to the high branch
of the neighbor's Arizona Ash.

Hummingbirds hover
then lunge for a red feeder
to sip of the home-made nectar.

I watch, drink green tea,
drop cookie crumbs
for a battalion of sugar ants.

Tortilla Shrine of Our Lady
of Los Apaches Café

Opposing walls show staggered posters
in the tradition of the stations of the cross.
The one on Johnny Mata's left depicts a warrior
astride a fallen princess, long black hair
splayed on the clay between his feet.

The waitress brings the puffy taco special;
Johnny swallows a mixture of refried beans,
crisp light shell, long tender threads
of chicken breast, christened with Crisco,
homemade salsa and maternal heart.
Sweat streams, temple to his neck.

Fragrant cumin reminds him of his mother's cousin,
trips to her Monterrey home. Mestizo looks,
her musk perfume, his raw heart.
His head tilts, eyes close, recovers the memory
curled up in the refuge of his mother's gaze.

Coils in the upholstered bench collapse,
the shock scatters oleander petals

onto the buttered tortilla beside his plate.
By twos and threes they paint La Malinche's image,
she ascends the poster on a ladder of wind.

The cafe owner built the tortilla shrine the next day.
A placard beneath the poster tells an account,
a woman's voice whispered just before Johnny left.

Yes my love, I am Mexico.
You have suckled at my bosom since birth.
Praise me, not virgin or vision,
even when history's memory lacks faith.

Pain Demands We Laugh

Your body a sculpture of broken bones,
pulleys suspend your arms and legs.
A morphine IV drips, monitors flash and beep.

I presume myself persona non grata,
guilt-ridden,
knowing had I been there two nights before,
wire would not lock your jaw.

You managed to find the scrap of fender
fastened by baling wire. A bonfire's comfort
left behind along with a litany of empties;
beer cans, bags of chips, a one-quart lighter fluid tin.

Loud music provoked rebellion from the shadows,
One song warned; *The boys are back in town.*
Another declared; *Baby we were born to run.*
Your penultimate act foretold by a car stereo.

A cushion of south Texas soil,
fresh plowed and fertile,
kept the tractor from taking your life.

The cartoon coyote survived such stunts
when we were young.
He wore a tire tread banner off a cliff
to the canyon far below.
The kind of humor boys appreciate
because it hurts.

At your bed rail, absent appropriate tears
I presume muffled profanities
offer the chance to console, express regret.

Instead your stainless steel grin shakes me
and as is custom, pain demands we laugh.

Dead Grackle Directions

I look down waiting at a traffic signal
to see a grackle on the curb
framed in a line of feathers and blood.

Hunger brought us both to this place.
He misjudged one hop,
eye trained on a puddle of crumbs,
beak ajar struck down between pecks.

The crossing signal light says walk,
I turn in the direction
of his outstretched broken wing.

Walk Away

People say I am a mistake without a home,
ignorant, going no where at all.
No one asks why I say nothing in reply.
If you need to know me by what I say,
walk away. I will be here when you are ready

to know the truth. Take a chance,
give me more than a flirty smile, you grow
just enough courage to hold my hand
for a little while, tell me I will find love
one day but I know you are wrong.

What you say you do not mean,
touch says it all, yours is so cold.
I'll be here when you are ready
to know truth. What I really mean
is walk away, walk away.

I know who I am, how honest love
feels. Fake words take me no where;
words lie all the time. Sour looks
play on simple minds. Walk away,
stay away cold touch. I will be here

with my legitimate truth.
What I really mean
is walk away, walk away.

Bedtime Story

A movie marquee comes into view
through the windshield of an old truck,
neon light reflected in curbside puddles
and the glint of a small girl's eye.

It's a bicycles handlebar I grip,
the truck a lie my eyes conjured
to confuse the journey from then to now.

I lock the bike in the basement
next to a radiator outside the men's room.
My way back to the lobby blocked
the only way out a tiny window
I reach on a trash can turned upside down.

Outside I find myself in a dark alley
encircled by a pack of stray dogs.

> Oh yes, now I remember.
> This isn't a story, it was a dream.

Now prepare for a new story,
to return to the battle in that narrow alley.

But wait,

The schoolyard bully appears in the distance,
In the spot I last saw the pack of wild dogs.

Return to the dream magic story maker.
But tonight, conjure a more hopeful dawn.

Pointing Chins

My neighbor wears a hard hat
I'm in a suit and silk tie.
We push our carts through H-E-B,
crossing paths in the beer aisle
we point our chins
at each other's heart.

Purposed to mend potholes,
trucks haul asphalt and tar
onto our lunar landscaped street.
They arrive before dawn to eat
tacos, pancakes and donut holes
at the corner coffee bar.

The sun sets behind
a power line horizon. Cast eyes
above the first layer of stars
and forget those unpaid bills,
that broken-down car.

A loud noise can be a wreck
or shots fired. All I care?
Can kids sleep in the discord

of sirens and flashing light?

The boy sprouts a middle finger
from the bud of his fist. The school bus
takes him away when the lights change.
Yet his nagging snarl robs my sleep.

The evening news, abandoned malls,
suburbs and seductions
more expensive than education
suggest another trip to H-E-B
to point chins at other hearts.

Incoherent Dreams

Tires hum along toll road and the singer
on the radio murmurs a poem I thought mine.
An exit ramp spills me on frontage road.
The sense of it stirs up similar journeys
to the home of another life lived far away –
where she lived, sometimes as I knew her,
other times in disguise.

Once as Ally Sheedy, the St. Elmo's Fire version.
Diabolical, charming; at war with all things bland.
So it came as no surprise she knocked on my door
in a swimsuit on a cold winter's day,
straight from the beach, tropical oil sheen,
sand on her toes, knuckles and knees.

The tortilla warmer full with yesterday's meal
on the verge of microwave combustion,
burns fingers after a two-minute carousel ride.

My neighbor sold me the warmer in a yard sale.
She looks like Sophia Loren and keeps
her "no one knows" cash in a coffee tin

flanked by essence of aloe hand cream
and a jar of dry roasted nuts.

Her point of view in line with my aunt on laundry day,
wood clothes pins pinched between her lips
on the left and scandals streaming from the right.

A stroll on the boardwalk, cold water, fruit cups.
Startled looks from tourists break the seal of my sleep.
The nightmare reminds there is no rest from sleep
while daytime routines wound like rusted daggers.
The hazy space between obligations is where
I harvest truth from fields of incoherent dreams.

Laundry Day

My feet rest on clean towels
cornered between old movies,
corn-stalk palms
and curtain pleats.

Static magnetizes dryer sheets
to pant legs, dark socks
to dress shirts,
stray hair strands
to pillowcase.

The sofa covered with spring
scented whites, dark clothes
and campaign promise;
I will not sleep until all are folded
and tucked away

Concert for Kites

A lightning storm on the Delaware River,
front seat ten stories high; the Philly side.
Benjamin Franklin Bridge the opening act.
Two miles of anchors, cables and steel
suspend cycles of pulsating light
framed by spider vein lightning strikes.

Rain and giant thunderclap cracks,
strobe effects freeze clouds,
windows recoil from wind shear
and the weight of God's kiss.

A pole tethered flag whips free
from its Jersey shore refuge.
chases summer storm in search
of a key, kite string and encore.

St. Paddy's Day

On a St. Paddy's Day jaunt around town,
clover green doors of an Irish pub
most difficult to resist.
A bar's name engraved on heavy plank,
Gothic letters painted gold.

Laughter rises to etched tin
and volleys to varnished parquet floors.
equal portions of perfume, tobacco and beer.

Seated in front of the stage, feet and fingertips
beat in time, strum of guitar and mandolins,
the barmaid dances a jig, red-hair swishes on her back.

An errant toe trips her and a pint of ale
on a frail looking lad. She embraces his pout.
Taunts disguise jealous eyes. All are forgiven
except barkeep, guilty of nabbing untended brews.

Sauntering on Smith St.

Walking to work makes good sense
with only sixteen city blocks between
apartment and workplace cubicle stall.
Suburban folk cast stones
into the clearing of my belief,
cite heat, humidity, unpredictable rain,
vagrants, the infamous downtown blight.

I test the mythical hoax disguised
in a mask of blank stares
and rubber soled shoes, sauntering
the sidewalks of Smith Street.

The major portion is one-way streets,
pedestrians and mounted patrols.
Horses hold their riders nobly
compared to carriage horses
wearing blinders and air of chagrin.

Alabaster, chromium, and 20th century
steel towers peer down on undulating
pavement, weeds and construction sites
that rise in my path like an abscess

every two or three steps. Footprint
haloes mapped to memory for the daily
springtime commute.
In summer, I ride the bus.

Three Lines

Strangers with something to prove
stand out from the start. They recite dogma
of sub-cultures, wear eccentric eyeglasses,
tend to argue content over form.

In the fifth hour of a six hour workshop,
three lines rearrange in mid-air,
chiseled by remarks from the fringe.
Excess cliches excised like a case of blight.

My left brain and Lorca's ghost
dive in to help me out. If I remained home,
this moment belongs to someone else.
If I left after lunch, the end never starts.

Lawns, Dogs and Refried Beans

Speak to me of manicured lawns, surrounded by hardpan,
dogs chained at opposite ends of yard. The scene reeks
of going to grandma's house, a food memory déjà vu
right before the waiter recites the daily special;
vegan Spanish rice, grilled chicken, cucumber
and jicama salad, and he calls it a Mexican plate.

I saw him drive up in a red Dodge Charger,
it reminds me of Bobby's 1969 440 Magnum;
airfoil, glass packs and mag wheels. We heard
it was stolen the night of the prom, stripped
and left on blocks in a nearby field. Tell me
of mariachis outside the church, la Quinceanera

in a circle of cousins, aunts and altar boys
in their black and white gowns. My altar boy
friends drank wine before the last mass.
The priest smudged ash on the bottle, the gap
between his mark and fruit of the vine
was enough to ban them from serving funerals

for cash and time out of class. Listen to this;

I set the chained dogs free. Silenced them
first with a make believe bone. They sniffed
their dog house border, ignored the open gate
and curled round their empty water bowls.
The complementary chips and salsa

have more character than the lunch special.
No beans, no refried beans! They served
eggs benedict at the end of the senior prom.
Altar boy buddies skipped to feast on menudo
and a keg of beer. The police strolled
into the back yard, found my friend's parents

and asked them to keep the noise down.
We gave them a plate of tamales, rice
and refried beans. Food transfigures fear,
turns scary looking cops into men who look
ordinary; they could be cousins for all I know.
Yes I'm talking about the guys in blue, guns

holstered in patent leather. One of them laughed
when the family pet, a dog named Rusty,
stood on his hind legs to dance. Holy Communion
wine tastes like high school nights in the backyard
seated in crooked circles. St. Augustine green
crushed to hardpan by the time the keg ran dry.

I prefer grape juice over wine for communion.
White bread, grape jelly, a taco on the side.
Same thing my grandmother served after I did my chores.

Part III - The Grace Escape

The Flavor of Gin

Sensuality boils in a cauldron
of wandering impulse.
Play games with me,
speak in the language of rain,
challenge thought, refuse deceit,
press your shoulder to mine,
a shower of fire and body salts.

Locked like Velcro
under summer sheets,
an aroma of compost,
skin – the flavor of gin.
Seduction a marble pillar
pulverized by dawn's first light.

Color of Memory

The bygone lover in red
demanded my affection,
stroked poetry
out of my skin. Shocked
prayer card Jesus
observant from His shelf.

Without her vibrant red,
blue forgets to breathe,
green is powerless to grow,
yellow does not yearn.

She prances innocent
in my dreams, emotion
thrown at her feet.
Reality fuses to myth,
arms wrap around her waist,
she turns to vapor
in mid-embrace.

Flavor of regret
corrupts memories,
the red dawn,

a mockingbird's
morning song.

At the crossroads of piety
and chagrin, I weep like violins
playing music without color.
The blood in my word body,
scrambled letters bruised black.

No One to Blame

blame rises like an arctic sun
revealing wasted time run empty
a sewer of blame

back long ago the other day
wasn't looking didn't hear you
must have misunderstood didn't you say
show tell give me clearly what you meant
it's all your fault don't you see

you have yourself to blame for the failure
the unanswered phone call missed opportunity
if only you would try harder be smarter listen
do what you're told not waste your money

keep telling you and you never listen
never hear bad words poor health
blame yourself not me told you
one day you'd suffer get sick
emasculate in shame

helped you see the light
the switch the path you couldn't see

why because I give of my heart my dreams
last can of beans sitting here alone
old tired cold afraid you'll never know

for all your damn it to hell romantic love
can never sell make a dime find a cure
all because you're to blame
you and all the others
hiding in tents of blame

Depression for Dessert

Baked beans and franks
for dinner, a sparsely
furnished room. The empty
can and illegal supply
of prescription relief
by the sink. The man said;
Just one before bed
will put you right to sleep.
The sun is 45 degrees away
from touchdown,
I'm in no mood to wait.

One for dessert
brings no peace of mind.
A second serving elicits
a deeper sense of doom.
Anxiety is uncontrolled,
erasing luxurious sleep.
The last pill is served
on a paper plate with graham
crackers and near frozen milk.
The crispness of each cinnamon
flavored bite is a loud crunch,

I sink to the floor
to finish the whole box. Air

from the open refrigerator
pours out like liquid nitrogen.
At the precipice of resignation,
one voice shouts from the void.
Get off the floor! Intestines spasm,
feels I've been kicked in the groin.

Lights from a car in the parking lot
pierce my eyes. The mercy of cold
linoleum pushes toward porcelain,
a two-finger stab. Death flushes out,
all that remains, dry heaves
and stench. An odor that wakes me
at dawn like a disconsolate friend.

Closet Space

Your former lovers
confront me
on move-in day.

Tokens of obsession
similar to mine
sit on shelves
in your walk-in closet.

Our new space polluted
with men from your past.

Please move them out,
I need room for my shirts.

Empty Kiss

Background music,
her hand reaches out.
Incidental touch. Sit
back, move, avoid
organic response.
Kisses, light strokes.
Is this a demon
or guardian angel?
Conceal turmoil,
a macho veneer.
Undone buttons
expose passion,
a siege of retreat.
I eat her kiss, vacuous,
no moisture, no hint
of intent. Because a kiss
means something else
after foul names
were brought into the room.

Disposable Love Song

Discount bookstore poetry,
authors arranged alphabetically,
A hardback edition of The Prophet
by Kahlil Gibran catches my eye.

Inscribed on page one;
From Steve to dear Marita.
A greeting card love song
nestled inside the back flap.

Gibran's Prophet begins with love
and ends with a farewell.
His premonition comes full circle;
Marita ransomed her heart
for fast food cash
and a John Grisham paperback.

Ambition

Connected cubes filled with rabid egos
arrange credenzas with pictures,
mementos, little Mikey's trophy.

Daily routines directed
by chief executive greed.
Shadows proclaim the hot and hip
campaign, up the ante
defining bottom line.
Everything homogenized
except the catchy jingle.

Consumers eagerly exhaust personal savings
oblivious to the cycle of depression and debt
until friends and neighbors are swallowed
by a pit of pink slips after last quarterly report.

A fast track executive races to refuge
on blood-soaked tracks,
pulls in for a pit stop,
fills an empty dream tank
as gaudy network dribble
numbs the brain.

Futility is the champion
in this endless chase,
the checkered flag never falls.

banging throb
tremors
on the heels
of bombs

prayers for sleep
sheets of sob

tablet tree
chemical freeze
remove the sting

one eight-ounce glass
foil wrapped pills

scarce comfort seeds
roll under chair
chased on all fours

a junkie's air
hung over
wrung out
confused

Their messages translate in lion speak,
my animal spirit tongue,
conversations expand beyond domestic design
into the realm of pop culture, our favorite dreams.

Spooky curls in my lap as Brandy climbs
behind the sofa, rests on my shoulder
then grooms my hair with her barbed tongue.

Slow fingertip strokes, skullcaps to rigid tails,
I am mesmerized by a symphony of purrs.

Their company pacifies my restless mood,
poised to boil over; relieved, as my hostess
appears at the door.
in sequins, sapphires and sass.

Wet Sand Fingerprints

We walk the shore
under the candle of an indigo moon,
a plastic bag of empty bottles dangle
more resonant than tubular bells.
Bonfire embers glow by the surfside bar.
A rock ledge embankment, our seat under the stars.

Plans of ancient ruin tours are the cure
to survive long tropical nights. Breaking surf
never stops preaching its foreign tongue.
A cruise ship at the pier blocks shrimp boats,
throws blinking red light at the sky
like pebbles into a placid lake.

I abandon the fallacy of shooting stars,
open another dulce de leche confection,
devour it in two vice-like bites,
a tower of cellophane wrappers at my feet.

Sand the texture of silk pajamas cradles
my empty agua fresca and calloused heels.

You lean toward my face, my nostrils

against your cheek, your hair in my teeth,
we exchange candied whispers, sweet as mango.

Seagulls cackle at sunrise as the tide comes ashore.
We laugh ourselves upright,
branded by terrycloth tattoos
and wet sand fingerprints.

Bandages

Wounds curdle a string of crimson pearls.
Blood sutures like linchpins, iodine drenched,
skin the color of rust, white gauze glued to skin,
butterfly bandage binds broken edge, one to the next.

Diseased minds hide under a veneer surface,
neglected as moss on bark under a pile of wood.
Depression is blue, gunmetal cold, belligerent;
as opposed to the color of a sky,
refracting the sun's full range of light.

One odd brother, sister, uncle or aunt; in every family
there is at least one. Poor thing, whispered over coffee,
disparaging glances like poison darts.

Patients exit emergency rooms, infections under control.
Scars fade, inkless tattoo treasured as Purple Hearts.

Undressed wounds do not heal, scabs rip away,
a new string of crimson hardens
in the furrow of shrunken flesh.

Unmistakable disorders of imbalanced minds

simmer in grocery store isles,
office cubicles, neighborhood bars.
Nameless beings that look a lot
like your brother, sister, uncle or aunt.

Part IV - Faith is a Verb

The Resolute Dawn

An alarm set by God's hand.
Prayers reveal His word
between gaps
of malnourished slumber,
last dreams, grains
of ocular sand.
I resist the day's demands,
double espresso in hand, sip
silent morning revelations,
surrender my will to receive
a measure of wisdom
I cannot claim as mine.

A measure of wisdom
my ego does not resist.
A measure of wisdom
God provides at dawn's first light.

Patron Saint of Broken Vows

Gabrielle's cape, royal purple on the original seventh day, now faded, a moth-eaten puce, shrouds her soiled wings. Stoic eyes take in everything, examining the atmosphere ranging from despair to depravity. Leathery arms gesticulate in disgust. She commands servants to cater marzipan to the feet of quiescent saints.

Armies of warrior cherubs return from fugitive planets, vomit pools of lost souls. Buster's slow dance in the vitriolic bog arouses Gabrielle's intent. She hails the smallish boy nursing a heroin cocktail enmeshed in the illusion of maternal breast. Buster rabidly kicks, paces like a cornered prisoner, Gabrielle seductively sings; *What are you up to my Monday child so fair of face?*

The chink of the door echoes as The Lord bursts across the threshold, plods up to the purple devil. Smoothing his solid chartreuse suit, the Lord says; *This morsel finds absolution in a needle, that is why I've set him free.* St. Peter arrives in a panicked state, tap-taps his Rolex, motions to the Lord. *Gabrielle replies; this junkie is pure sin in a room of sinner's redeemed, he belongs to me.*

With a resigning nod the Lord says, let it be.

Day of the Dead Moon

Nourish the dead with ritual,
processions under the lazy light
of a rising moon, luminescence
permeates flesh. A checkerboard
field, headstone and statue markers,
centuries of visits carve a stone path.

Life nourished by a reason
to feast. A cantina jukebox blares,
laughter, dance and drink spill
into a papel picado framed courtyard,
under the seductive glow of a neon moon.

Pan de los muertos, marigolds, cold beer,
candy skulls and snapshots in a shoe box,
carried to ancestor's graves; nourish
memory with rituals of the dead.

Ofrendas invite sinners and saints
under the yellow spell of candlelight.
Song, calaveras and copal blend
and rise in the hazy November night.

Angelitos and masked dancers escort
away the dead to end the celebrations,
death nourished with authentic ritual
under the blue light of a full moon.

House of Prayer

Let me build a house of prayer,
one pew where you and God sit alone.
Planks bone polished, smooth as moonstone.
Stained glass windows beyond compare.

Time waits outside, no worries or care.
Silence subdues you, monk-like.
In that place, he makes His word known.

When you face burdens too heavy to bear
behold My son Jesus, pierced by rusty spike.
By His cross He ascended My throne.

Seed of Praise

Accumulate the seasons since time began
and create from this a seed.
In corners and corridors I worship with a glad heart
and joyous song the hope born of that seed,
fed by my maker, my gracious shepherd.
I am filled with joy for what he gives his people.

Fed by the atom of the first sun.
That called to the first plant.
That brought forth the first sprout.
That shed light on the first blossom.

I join the church in thanks and praise;
for the beauty of that flower pales in contrast
to the birth of the spirit,
the ecstasy of cultivating lives turned from sin.

Life's struggle creates poise and strength,
His good blessing of love and faith;
transforms the weight of a cross into light
and gifts that endure all seasons.
All who know Him share my joy.

Do not forsake the light of His love
Come join the chorus of believers
who receive His favor,
for he is good, worthy of worship
and never-ending songs of praise.

Picnic Bench Constellation

My hands look like paternal grandfather's,
he custom built cabinets from press board,
pine, iron-forged tools and spit,
blue veins rippled
 on the back of my hand when he died.

The rest of my anatomy is a mystery. Scars
show where the collective joy, profanity, whiskey,
blood and sweat of Motecuhzoma, Santa Ana,
Juarez and Zapata enter and exit at will.
Their ashes whistle through Bald Cypress.
Gusts make each tree sing its own dirge.
The melody draws sap from limb, rock and man;
turns to crystal, reflects the morning sun.

Dew drops hold prayers muttered in whispers
among pillars of faith. This outdoor temple resounds,
a choir of mockingbird, grackle, duck and goose.
Streaks of grey scale excrement paint abstract tears
on a picnic bench. Incense from charcoal brick
and lighter fluid spiral toward heaven;
praise be to mothers, compadres, a nice cut of meat.

Mesquite trees know more about being
than I have learned in 600 full moons. A treasure
wrapped in white light, the tail of a child's kite,
the net of a fisher of humankind.

Under Tall Trees

Wildflowers and weathered screen doors
decorate the slope aimed at the hidden stream
live oak and mesquite kept secret. Brown sleeps
under the sage bush, no complaints,
without compunction for painting the grass dead.

Smoke ribbons through tall trees furloughed
by an outdoor grill that remembers hot coals
like a ghost who remembers her daughter's laugh.

Envious shade, the spoiled child, conceals primal hues
with a somber-tipped brush. Red wine ripples
in a stemware bowl while blue and yellow
use butterfly wings to paint the slope green.
Fingertips weave whispers, sighs and sacred touch
in the pores just cleansed of regret. The hidden stream

renders an acoustic version of Eric Clapton's Layla. Lovers
dance in circles on a flagstone deck under tall trees
that mimic a kaleidoscope swirling light, arthritic branches,
a bird house and brown leaves against a honeybee hive.

The mockingbird perched on a high branch shifts

its pointed song from clouds in pantomime
of the running of the bulls to locals speeding past
the hidden gate. Unexpected tires creep over crushed
granite. The newlyweds glide across the green slope
blue and yellow use to avoid the noise of being found.

Impulse and clarity slumber in the circle of shade
rendered sacred by burnt offerings of stockpiled regret
on wildflower altars, a fragrance like sage ribbon ornaments.

Songbirds on a dusky perch, wings well spent, compose
lullabies on the hidden stream's music sheet. Their whispers
ribbon through fields of yellow wildflowers, past
the hidden blue stream, low-slung green slope and echo
vows exchanged under the tall trees of a Texas Spring.

Kristin

Hazel eyes reflect light
like polished jade.
A voice filled with discovery.

Beauty, infused with a fire
from the Holy Spirit, inspires a poet
to search out new words.

Blessed heart, warm as a whisper,
bright as a star's corona, unbound,
fearless, shared without ration.

Integrity strong as diamond
faceted by the blade
of dreams and distress.

Humbly obedient, God's will
pursued before your own,
He delights in your daily prayer.

And when you laugh,
I hear wind chimes,
thin-piped fairy bell pings

a repeating refrain;
passion, purpose, best friend,
my beautiful devoted wife.

Before you, days were routine,
nights obscured by the lies of pursuit.
Dark times, in the absence of hope.

I saw with eyes shut tight;
stars, moon and midnight shadows.
Waterfalls drop into a sea of trees.
Oceans dance on the surf.
Lightning veins turn night to day.

I heard in the silence of isolation
bird song in a sunset sky.
Children laugh on a merry go round.
The gentle murmur of summer rain.
Whistling winds in an open field.

I felt with still hands
the cool flow of a mountain stream.
Warm sand touched by summer sun.
The soft fur of a newborn pup.
A tingle from the kiss of new love.

Now I live in the light

He shines through you,
and I see with eyes wide open.
I hear in the company of a choir.
I feel the promise of your hand in mine.

Labor and Prayer

In all things Lord, help our labor serve others
even when slighted, powerless and without hope.
Forgive us when we subordinate your word,
when workplace pressure is used as excuse
to ignore the message to love our enemies,
(disenfranchised, neglected and souls
inserted in our paths) as we love ourselves.

Lord, help our knowledge and skills guide
those who rely on regular paychecks. The ones
without influence in their workplace. Those limited
due to insufficient education and weak economies.
Souls who suffer from histories
of poor choice and weak resolve.

We strive to promote faith in pursuit of alternatives
that glorify You. Help us serve those without integrity
in ways that reflect the light of your love.
Help us serve Lord, to honor and glorify your name,
to reflect the Holy Spirit's power in times of distress.

Lord, help us find word and action to share
with those of little power in the workplace.

We grow large in number, our labor
a yoke of great burden. Help us rise above
our selfish acts. Help us discern your will
and design for our lives when corporate
authority intrudes with our ability to do right.

We recognize our service is meant for all people;
clients who rely on our skills, customers
who look to us for help, the sick in need of healing,
families protected by the homes we've built.
Help us share love to honor, respect, obey
and carry out our workplace commands
even when spite darkens our heart.
Let our best labor be our most perfect prayer.

In Christ's name we pray. Amen.

ACKNOWLEDGEMENTS

Grateful acknowledgement is made to the editors of the following publications, where versions of some of the poems first appeared:

BorderSenses: Seeds on My Chin, Tortilla Shrine of Our Lady of Los Apaches Café;

Wild Goose Poetry Review: Concert for Kites

Arch and Quiver: The Flavor of Gin

Very special thanks to the staff and artists of Gemini Ink in San Antonio, Texas for their dedication to making creative writing workshops available to all writers. I am grateful to all the workshop leaders and visiting poets especially Cyrus Cassells, Li-Young Lee, Kevin Young, Ed Hirsch, Barbara Ras and Dale Marie Rogers. Their insight and guidance helped me grow in my poetry.

Rudy Martinez Jr. was born in San Antonio Texas and educated at The University of Texas at San Antonio. He has spent his career as a CPA in accounting and business while writing poetry as a means of creative expression. He currently lives with his wife Kristin in Spring, Texas. They have a blended family of two sons, two daughters and four grandsons. This is his first collection of poems.

The setting for "Learning for the Licensed" is the San Antonio Convention Center where continuing education courses were held for CPA's in rooms large enough to hold over 1,000 people.

La Malinche in "Tortilla Shrine of Los Apaches Café" is one of the most controversial figures of the Spanish Conquest, the woman also known as Doña Marina (ca. 1500-1527?) was one of Hernando Corté's trusted counselors. As the mother of a son and daughter of mixed blood, the same mestizo blood that courses through most Mexicans, Doña Marina may rightfully be considered the Mother of the Mexican Nation.

"Walk Away" is a collaboration with my son Nathaniel Vincent Martinez Sr. He wrote the chorus of a song that became the concept of the poem.

H-E-B in "Pointing Chins" is one of the largest grocery chains in Texas.

"Kristin" is dedicated to my wife Kristin Martinez; "Scars" is dedicated to my brother Raymond Martinez, the unfortunate injured party of the poem.